SCENARIO
QUEEN

God is omnipresent and omnipotent;
He never slumbers or fails.

Roberta Jackson

ISBN 978-1-64492-942-1 (paperback)
ISBN 978-1-64492-944-5 (digital)

Christian Faith Publishing, Inc.
832 Park Avenue
Meadville, PA 16335
www.christianfaithpublishing.com

All scriptures, unless otherwise stated, are taken from the New International Version of the Holy Bible.

Printed in the United States of America

Contents

Acknowledgments

First and foremost, I thank God almighty for saving me through the years! I thank Him for His steadfast love and destiny for my life.

To my four blessings from God:

My wonderful husband, Tyrone. You are my biggest critic and greatest support. You have shown me what an accomplished dream chaser looks like. Thank you for believing in me, time and time again, when I didn't see it and for not allowing me to settle. Thank you for loving me, cheering me on, and pushing me on to fulfill my dream! I love you to life!

My sons Tommie Grant, III and Isaac Grant, thank you for your love, assertive encouragement and endless support. Thanks for believing in me and thinking that I'm the best. I love you more! I pray you both see me as an example for you to use your many gifts and talents for God's glory!

My grandson Jordan Grant, thank you for your curious mind, witty support and loving heart. Never stop writing, singing or dreaming and keep expanding your mind with knowledge. I love you!

Special thanks and dedication goes to my mother, Frankie Robertson. You believed when others had no clue, you gave me my first dictionary and a book named *Writing Well*. You said the first time you held me, I looked up at you with my big eyes, with my hand on your arm and I started smacking like I had so much to say. Then one week before you passed away, you told me that you could see God using me! Here I go. I wished you could have been here to see this book came to life. I Love You! Rest in peace, Mama.

My sister Vickie and cousin Lori, thank you for your support, your enthusiasm, and for your help in proofing my handiwork. You are the best!

Finally, thanks to my daddy Isaac Robertson, the rest of my family and friends that have cheered me on through the years and for their continued prayers. I love and truly appreciate each and every one of you!

Introduction

In life there are a lot of explainable and unexplainable things that happen on a daily basis. But your belief in whether there is or isn't a God will determine how you will or will not respond.

This book is for those who do not believe that God truly exists and only believe that things just happen by chance. This book is also for those who believe that God truly exists and know their steps are ordered by the Lord.

"The Lord makes firm the steps of the one who delights in him." (Ps. 37:23)

During our journey through life, we have all had encounters where a few seconds made a difference. For some, missed or delayed transportation saved your life. For others, out of nowhere, a still small voice whispered something to you and kept a bullet or car from harming you.

We have so many stories to tell if we all would just be honest with ourselves. But because we live in such a tangible world where we have to see it with our eyes or touch it with our hands, anything else would be unthinkable because of the lingering fear that someone would think that we were a little crazy or strange to admit such stories.

All the while, some of you are unaware of a loving Father who is watching over you because He is a God that loves you so much and wishes no harm to you. In His own way and timing, He's making Himself known to you. So will you acknowledge God and answer back?

This book contains stories to show whether in disobedience, youthful zeal, minding your own business, letting your guard down, or carelessness, God is always a strong tower in time of need. We don't deserve His unmerited love, endless grace, tender mercies, and undeniable protection. We could never do anything to earn or deserve it! But that is just the way He is because He loves us to death!

"For God so loved the world that he gave his one and only Son, that whoever believes in him shall not perish but have eternal life." (John 3:16)

Let the Scenarios begin…

CHAPTER 1

Angels on Wheels

Sometimes, that which seems so harmless may very well be the thing that takes you out!

Can you say "high school freshman"?

June couldn't believe how fast the past three years had gone by, and this was the end of summer break before she entered into the halls of Praise High School. Wow! She was beside herself with excitement entering the next phase of her life. June looked forward to playing JV sports. She said, "Freshman year, here I come!"

Her friend April was a junior at Praise High. She knew the ropes and planned on telling June all she needed to know about high school.

April was going up to Praise High on Wednesday to see her boyfriend practice on the varsity football team. April asked June if she wanted to go.

The answer was easy. "Do I stay home and be bored or go with my friend? Hmm… Hard choice, you think?"

On Wednesday, April picked up June in her two-door Kia. They rode along with the music blaring and excitedly talked about who would be at the practice. They were less than two minutes from the school. Then everything changed in a matter of seconds.

April and June started down the hill going pretty fast into the first curve which turned to the left. The two wheels on the passenger side of April's car lifted slightly off the ground. June started praying, and she didn't want April to know she was scared.

The next curve to the right came up, and the car lifted slightly on the two driver's side wheels. June kept praying. As April and June approached the next curve going toward the left, they had gained momentum. By now, the car was lifted higher and driving only on the two driver's side wheels.

June heard the tires screeching, she screamed, "Slow down!"

By then, it was too late. They were crossing over the solid double lines and going into the other lane on two wheels. June's side was now in the air, and as she looked ahead, all she could see was the telephone pole they were going to hit head on. Then June saw a car speeding from around the corner toward them. They both screamed, and June yelled out loud, "God! Help!"

At that moment, it's like everything went into slow motion. April's hands quickly came off the steering wheel. As they came closer to the telephone pole, the car turned slowly back to the right while it was still on two wheels. At the same time, the car heading toward them appeared to be at a standstill, like something was holding it back.

As they were just inches from the oncoming car, April's car went *boom* as it landed back onto all four wheels and quickly swerved away from the oncoming car! During the whole time, April's hands were still clearly off the steering wheel. Once her car crossed over in front of the other car, it started going straight and then April grabbed the steering wheel with both hands.

There was one small curve remaining and then they were at Praise High. April and June drove into the driveway, parked right in front of the football practice, and they sat in silence. As they sat, June's thoughts were louder than the blaring music in the car.

After a couple of minutes, April turned off the car and jumped out to walk to the fence near the practice to talk to her boyfriend.

As for June, she was still in shock. She got out and sat on the car's hood and thought, *Coming to see this football practice, meeting people or looking at the new high school just doesn't seem interesting anymore after seconds earlier of having a close call with death.*

June ran the whole scene through her mind over and over again. She couldn't explain it and thought of various scenarios of what should have happened: *Their car should've flipped over. They should've been wrapped around the telephone pole. The other car should've hit them head on. There's no way April's car should've driven like that by itself and then we walk away untouched. Our parents should be getting calls right now about two fatalities.*

To the human mind, what happened to April and June was impossible, even Hollywood could not touch it. They thought their lives were up, but God stepped in and showed them: "He's not done with us!"

Food for thought

What memory or memories came to mind as you read this story? It's so amazing how two people could go through the same experience yet responds so differently; however, one point of view is not greater than the other.

Have you ever experienced something at the same time with someone else, and you both saw it totally differently or responded differently when it was over? How did it make you feel? Have you ever been going through something and you called out to God and you witness His hand intervening on your behalf on the spot?

Scriptures for your soul

> Then Moses stretched out his hand over the sea, and all that night the Lord drove the sea back with a strong east wind and turned it into dry land. The waters were divided, and the Israelites went through the sea on dry ground, with a wall of water on their right and on their left. (Exod. 14:21–22)

> I cried out to God for help; I cried out to God to hear me. When I was in distress, I sought the Lord; at night I stretched out untiring hands, and I would not be comforted. (Ps. 77:1–2)

For he will command his angels concerning you to guard you in all your ways; they will lift you up in their hands, so that you will not strike your foot against a stone. (Ps. 91:11–12)

So do not fear, for I am with you; do not be dismayed, for I am your God. I will strengthen you and help you; I will uphold you with my righteous right hand. (Isa. 41:10)

"For I know the plans I have for you," declares the Lord, "plans to prosper you and not to harm you, plans to give you hope and a future." (Jer. 29:11)

But the Lord is faithful, and he will strengthen you and protect you from the evil one. (2 Thess. 3:3)

CHAPTER 2

In the Nick of Time

*We all have choices in
life and each has consequences
and some may usher in you
needing a rescue.*

It was the beginning of a very boring hot summer in South Carolina. June anxiously waited to start her sophomore year. June and her best friend Denise each were the second of four children. They were inseparable, and you would think they were blood sisters.

Denise's family took summer vacations every year. June's parents were divorced and family vacations no longer existed. This year,

Denise asked June to go with her family on their summer vacation to Niagara Falls. Denise's youngest brother couldn't attend because of a summer football camp.

June was speechless and excited at the same time. She had never been out of South Carolina before and hoped her mom would let her go.

When she got home, June asked her mom, and she said yes. With excitement, June screamed for joy and hugged her. She thought to herself, *In a couple weeks, I will be going on a* free *trip to Niagara Falls on a vacation with my friend and her family!* It couldn't come soon enough.

The days flew by. The night before the trip while June packed, it dawned on her— she was the first of her siblings to ever go to New York! Wow! This made the trip even sweeter.

As June was about to pack her last piece of clothing, her mother entered the room. She noticed the serious look on her mom's face. June's mood immediately changed from excitement to sadness and then she thought to herself, *Did Mom change her mind?*

Her mom said, "I know you will be staying at a hotel, and it will have a swimming pool. Do not pack your bathing suit! You know you can't swim."

Of course, being a teen, all June could think of was, *Mama's trying to spoil my fun, I will be okay.* June said, "But, Mama, Denise and her siblings are taking theirs!"

Her mama said, "I don't care. They can swim, and you cannot! You are my daughter, either you leave it, or you stay at home!"

June was in shock and thought, *How could she be so mean? Nothing would happen. Mama's spoiling my fun.* June said with hesitation, "Okay, Mama, I won't take it." She placed the bathing suit back into her drawer, and her mother left the room.

As she closed the suitcase June thought, *That's not fair! Nothing will happen to me! Denise's mother, father, and siblings will be there.* Then without an afterthought, June went back into her drawer and pulled out the bathing suit and hid it under her clothes in her suitcase—just in case her mama checked it later.

The next day as June waited for her ride, she had a heavy heart of guilt. On one hand, she hated disobeying her mother; and on the other hand, she didn't want to be left out of the fun. June rationalized her decision was "okay."

Her guilty feelings lasted for a while as she and Denise's family drove and even while conversations were going on in the car. But once they hit the North Carolina border, her mind could only think of all the fun they were going to have.

The road trip was so exciting! They made stops in each state: North Carolina, Virginia, West Virginia, and Pennsylvania. June had forgotten how great it felt to take road trips with her whole family.

Denise's parents decided to take it easy the third day in New York. Her father decided he wanted to relax by watching the television and everyone else wanted to go by the pool at the hotel. June knew this was coming.

As June took out her bathing suit, guilt slapped her right on the face! She could see her mother and hear her voice as clear as day. The conversation played over and over in her mind. But again, she rationalized her actions, and she slowly changed into her bathing suit.

Once at the pool, Denise's mother sat on the step in the water, and June sat in a chair. Denise and her siblings took off swimming effortlessly across the pool. June watched in awe for a couple of minutes. She had never been in a pool before, and she felt like a little kid full of excitement and curiosity. They were the only people at the pool.

June finally got brave enough to get into the pool and sit on the steps by Denise's mom. She started splashing her feet in the water and thought she was really doing something. But as June continued to watch everyone else swimming back and forth across the pool, laughing as they jumped off the side by the rope and back into the water, she felt left out. She wanted to have fun like everyone else. Boldness and adventure rose up in June. She got up and started slowly walking into the water and thought to herself, *This feels nice. I don't know what Mama was so worried about anyway.*

As June barely walked out into the water, Denise's siblings said, "Come on, June!"

She said, "No, I'm okay."

They were near the five feet rope that divided the pool. They swam some more and then came by June and said, "Come on, we'll walk with you. It's not that deep."

June looked out into the pool—it looked so cool and inviting. She reasoned to herself, *The rope is near the six feet mark. I'm more than five feet tall. I can make it to the rope.*

So they all started to walk out slowly with June. As she proceeded, she was soon startled by the pool floor slanting downward at an angle. But she couldn't let them know she was getting scared. But they somehow sensed June's reluctance so they urged her on, so she went on.

As June walked out a little further, she now noticed how the water was getting closer to her face, but she kept her eyes fixed on the rope. She knew she could make it. She was determined to make it to the rope.

Then it happened! June was more than half way to the rope, but the water was overwhelming as it came up higher on her face. She panicked! She knew she was going to drown, so she started screaming for help as the water went over her face. Denise and her siblings also panicked and swam away from June to the other side of the pool.

Watching from the poolside, Denise's mother started running back and forth screaming for help! At this moment, several thoughts flashed through June's mind. *I should've listen to Mama. I'm going to drown! I've got to reach the rope!*

June kept going under, reaching out toward the rope and each time she came up, she screamed for help! She was petrified as the pool floor kept slanting downward the more she walked forward. June kept thinking, *If I could make it to the rope, I will be okay.*

Time stood still for her, it seemed like she was in the water forever, and the rope kept getting further and further away no matter how hard she tried to reach it. Denise's mom kept running back and forth while screaming for help, and no one came.

June then had a feeling this would be her last time going under, and it would be over. She screamed one more time and went under thinking if only she could get to the rope. After that, it was a blur. But somehow she made it to the rope, pulled herself to the poolside, and lifted herself out of the pool!

June was exhausted, and her mind was racing, *What happened?* She glanced back at the rope and then at the steps and then from the rope to where she now sat and wondered, *How did I do it?*

Denise, her mother, and siblings came rushing over to June to make sure she was okay. They all hugged her and was thankful she made it out of the pool alive.

As they left the pool, June was overwhelmed with guilt for being so disobedient to her mother. As she looked at the pool in passing, it didn't look so friendly and inviting to her anymore. She now had a new respect for the pool and her mother.

June thought about what took place in the pool as they drove back home. She knew with all her heart that there was no way she could have saved herself by getting to the rope, have enough strength to pull herself along the rope, and then mustering up more strength to pull herself out of the water. She realized at that moment "Who" really saved her. Not flesh and blood, not her own weak flesh but a loving supernatural God who heard a young rebellious child's cry for help. Thank you, Lord!

Food for thought

What memory or memories came to mind as you read this story? Can you recall at least one time when you did something you knew you shouldn't have done, and you knew there should be instant consequences for it? But somehow, it never came and you made it to the other side. But you know in your gut, you shouldn't have. Then maybe, just maybe, God too came to you "in the nick of time"!

Scriptures for your soul

> Be strong and courageous. Do not be afraid or terrified because of them, for the Lord your God goes with you; he will never leave you nor forsake you. (Deut. 31:6)

Save me, O God, for the waters have come up to my neck. I sink in the miry depths, where there is no foothold. I have come into the deep waters; the floods engulf me. (Ps. 69:1–2)

But now, this is what the Lord says—he who created you, Jacob, he who formed you, Israel: "Do not fear, for I have redeemed you; I have summoned you by name; you are mine. When you pass through the waters, I will be with you; and when you pass through the rivers, they will not sweep over you. When you walk through the fire, you will not be burned; the flames will not set you ablaze.

Do not be afraid, for I am with you; I will bring your children from the east and gather you from the west." (Isa. 43:1–2, 5)

Surely the arm of the Lord is not too short to save, nor his ear too dull to hear. (Isa. 59:1)

Let us then approach God's throne of grace with confidence, so that we may receive mercy and find grace to help us in our time of need. (Heb. 4:16)

CHAPTER 3

Victory to Terror

The word says, "Money is the root of all evil." So what's the root of a loser's behavior?

June moved up to Praise High's girls varsity basketball team at the end of ninth grade as the seventh man. Her coaches saw something special in her.

At first, she wanted to stay on the JV team one more year because she had a bond with her teammates. June loved playing basketball almost as much as she loved running track, but deep down she knew it was an honor and a big deal.

Praise High was on a roll. The girls varsity basketball team just won another game. June's team was coming to the end of the season and had couple more games left to play. The team was having a really good season.

A few games into the season, Praise High played against Coward High School. Praise High beat them pretty badly, and Coward High wasn't too happy. Threats were made by some of the players on Coward High's team. They let Praise High know they would get them when they come to their school. But Praise High girls believed it was just "talk." The season went on and then it was time to go to Coward High before the city tournament.

D-day! When Praise High arrived at Coward High, there were students standing around outside as Praise High team got off the bus and walked down the steps into the gym. By the end of the evening, the Praise High's girls' and boys' teams played great games and won. Can you say "sweep"?

They were excited and celebrated all over Coward High's gym. After the win, Praise High's girls shook hands with Coward High's girls but some of them said in passing, "We're gonna get you, and you won't leave this gym alive!"

June thought, *What? Are they serious?* The same thing happened after the boys' game.

Once the boys' game was done, June looked around the gym and noticed there were a lot of cops in the gym. Some cops came over to her coaches and told them to have everyone sit down until they come back to escort them to the bus.

June started praying because she didn't know what was waiting for them behind the closed doors. The boys started talking junk about what they were gonna do if someone messed with them, but it was evident on their faces that they were scared too. The girls were clearly terrified. The coaches stood to the side whispering amongst themselves, and they looked really concerned. The cops left Praise High alone as they cleared the gym.

Out of nowhere, the door quickly opened, everyone thought it was the cops coming to get them. But they soon realized it was a student from Coward High. He peeked into the gym and started screaming profanity and then he threw something into the gym! Everyone instantly jumped up from the bleachers and ran further back into the gym while screaming for help!

The cops came and ran after the student. Then two other cops rushed in, closed the door behind them, and now they guarded it from the inside. Once the door was secured, they went over to see what was thrown into the gym and realized it was a "stink bomb" (a small ball that smells like a rotten egg). Thank God it didn't go off.

Afterwards, several more cops came in and one of them said, "The crowd has almost died down outside. I want everyone to stay together in a group 'til we get everyone on the bus. Don't fall behind. Walk in lines of three, one girl inside and one boy or a coach on the outside."

Some of the boys let out loud noises of disbelief and questioned the cop, "Why can't we be in the middle?" The cop gave them a look, and they shut up quickly and got in line as they were told.

Everyone was terrified by now; no one wanted to be the first three to walk out or the last three to exit the gym. The cops slowly opened the two gym doors. After peering out with caution, they gave the signal to proceed.

It was 9:00 p.m. and the area outside the gym was poorly lit. June felt like she was a soldier in Desert Storm surrounded by the enemy that laid in wait to ambush them as she looked yards away toward the twenty steps they had to go up to get to the bus. Several cops were all around them as they started on their quest to the bus. They were reminded by the cops after taking several steps, "Stay calm, don't run to the bus, and walk in a tight group."

They had to pass by small clusters of Coward High's students standing outside the gym. Some of these students started threatening and throwing trash at the Praise High's students as they passed them. Then out of nowhere, as they got closer to the steps, a stink bomb flew over the Praise High's students' heads from behind. Some cops took off after the students, some cops stayed and yelled, "Stay calm and keep moving!"

All the while, some students near the gym doors were still screaming out threats as the Praise High's students got further and further away from them.

June was in the middle of the pack. They all finally made it up the stairs with a small sigh of relief as they looked around and saw only the bus down the sidewalk. Suddenly, there was silence. No threats, no profanity—nothing! You could have heard a pin drop on the ground.

They were almost by the bus when a shout sprang out of the silence, "Get them!" Then rocks flew from all directions.

The Praise High's students screamed, and some girls started crying. At the same time, the coaches yelled, "Run to the bus!" Some students were pushed down and trampled on as they all made the mad dash to the bus.

It was chaos! Rocks flying; Coward High's students running and screaming profanity; cops running, yelling at the students; and Praise High's students running and screaming in terror while trying to get on the bus.

Once on the bus, the coaches told them to get down and lay on the floor. A lot of players were screaming, some were crying, all were shaking in fear of the unknown. The coaches tried their best to calm everyone down with the assurance that they were finally safe.

Then just as quickly as it started, it was over. No more rocks and no more profanity. Once the coaches felt it was safe on the bus, they told everyone to sit in their seats. The coaches did a head count and made sure everyone was okay.

It was a miracle; no one was hurt by the rocks or after being trampled on. But right outside the bus windows was madness as you saw police officers running after Coward High's students in the dark. It all seemed so surreal to June.

Once the police chief checked everything out, the bus was finally cleared to leave. Everyone just knew after such a traumatic experience that the police officers would escort them to the interstate. But they didn't.

As the bus pulled off, everyone was quiet, even the coaches. When the bus was totally away from the school, some of the boys started laughing and joking. Now they were tough and talking about what they would have done if they got hit by a rock. June sat silently in a seat by herself near the aisle in the middle of the bus and thanked God for His protection.

The bus passed a lot of houses before they got to the interstate. But right before the interstate's entrance lay a short unlit stretch of woods on both sides of the road. It's like everyone saw it at the same time, and there was silence on the bus again. It was so eerie, and you could feel the tension in the air as fear of what might happen once again entered everyone on the bus!

As the bus entered into the stretch of woods, June heard a calm voice whisper, "Duck!" For a split second she thought, *I've never experienced anything like this before. What's going on? I know the voice didn't come from behind me because girls are there.* She quickly lay down on her right shoulder and as she did, she heard a very loud crash from her window. Glass popped everywhere and then the loud crashing sound went straight through to the window on the other side of the bus. She started praying and rolled off her seat to the floor.

Everyone started screaming! After that rocks started flying nonstop from both sides of the road hitting the bus and busting out window after window after window! It sounded like a fireworks show that went terribly wrong. Then all of a sudden, the bus driver stopped in the middle of the street! Rocks were still flying! What's going on? Was the bus driver hit? Everyone screamed at the same time, "Keep going!" The bus driver took off! A few more rocks flew then the attack stopped, and an eerie silence fell.

The bus made it to the interstate. Once there, the bus driver radioed for help and the police came. The officers made sure everyone was okay. No one was seriously hurt; there were some small cuts from the popping glass. June wasn't scratched by any of the glass that rained over her seat. Once she got up, she realized the glass that popped all around her fell into the shape of her body on the floor.

Everyone was still in shock as they waited for another bus to pick them up. No one talked; you only heard crying of pain, of shock, of anger, of fear, and of disbelief. How could a game that everyone loved turned out to be so violent and maddening? What kind of people waited for an hour or beyond in the woods to ambush a bus? Who would've thought that morning when they woke up, this day would've ended not in victory but in such violence and terror?

When the bus arrived, everyone was scared to get on it. The cops surveyed the area and then they cautiously escorted them off the bus on to the other bus. Then they escorted them down the interstate a couple exits and then they were on their own. Once they made it back to Praise High School, it was truly a sight for sore eyes. But everyone was still traumatized by Coward High's students' behavior over losing two basketball games.

As June waited on her ride, her mind replayed that bus trip over and over. She couldn't help but realize how God spared her life. How He whispered to her to get down, and if she hadn't listened or acted quickly, then that first rock into the bus would've hit her. Knowing the force that carried it from one side of the bus to the other was enough to have killed her if it struck her head. June didn't know much about God, but she knew He loved her, her teammates, her coaches, and the bus driver enough to spare their lives that night.

Food for thought

What memory or memories came to mind as you read this story? Can you recall at least one time when you had to make a decision big or small, and you heard a soft voice telling you what to do or not to do? You knew deep within that was not your thoughts, and the voice couldn't have come from someone standing near you, if anyone was around. Can you now see that an all loving God was with you at a time that you didn't know Him? Or maybe a time you were shutting Him out and He still reached out to you because He loves you? Or even a time when you thought you were in charge and now you see it was God?

Scriptures for your soul

> Therefore let all the faithful pray to you while you may be found; surely the rising of the mighty waters will

not reach them. You are my hiding place; you will protect me from trouble and surround me with songs of deliverance. (Ps. 32:6–7)

Be merciful to me, my God, for my enemies are in hot pursuit; all day long they press their attack. My adversaries pursue me all day long; in their pride many are attacking me. When I am afraid, I put my trust in you. Then my enemies will turn back when I call for help. By this I will know that God is for me. In God, whose word I praise, in the Lord, whose word I praise in God I trust and am not afraid. What can man do to me? I am under vows to you, my God; I will present my thank offerings to you. For you have delivered me from death and my feet from stumbling, that I may walk before God in the light of life. (Ps. 56:1–3, 9–13)

He will cover you with his feathers, and under his wings you will find refuge; his faithfulness will be your shield and rampart. (Ps. 91:4)

I call on the Lord in my distress, and he answers me.

The Lord will keep you from all harm—he will watch over your life; the Lord will watch over your coming and going both now and forevermore. (Ps. 120:1, 121:7–8)

After the earthquake came a fire, but the Lord was not in the fire. And after the fire came a gentle whisper. (1 Kings 19:12)

Do not be afraid of those who kill the body but cannot kill the soul. Rather, be afraid of the One who can destroy both soul and body in hell. Are not two sparrows sold for a penny? Yet not one of them will fall to the ground outside your Father's care. And even the very hairs of your head are all numbered. So don't be afraid; you are worth more than many sparrows. (Matt. 10:28–31)

CHAPTER 4

My Guardian

Time and chance can happen to anyone, and you never know when you might need supernatural intervention.

June's family had only one car and lived in a new subdivision. It was a very nice and peaceful place to live. The neighbors that lived there were pretty close to one another. On a normal day, it's pretty deserted. But these days, with all the new homes going up, it's pretty hectic.

June had two very active toddler boys. Most days, they stayed indoors until late afternoon and then they would go outside and play in the yard.

June's husband left the house around noon to head to the car dealership to get some work done on the car. As he left, she noticed there was no sounds outside and once again they had sweet silence. But that could only mean that the construction workers were at lunch. So she was going to enjoy it while she could.

June and her children were watching *Sesame Street* in the living room. She sat in a chair that faced the front window. Twenty minutes later, she was alarmed when she saw a man quickly walking up her sidewalk toward the front porch. June was very cautious and very protective of her boys.

Seconds before she had just spoken to her children about calming down as they watched television. June heard the porch creek as the man stepped on it. She whispered softly to her children to be quiet. She wondered if he heard the television before she muted the sound or them talking. Quickly, she glanced down her empty driveway and saw his car parked in the street in front of her driveway. She started praying.

When June looked through the front door's peephole, she noticed how he was leaning on the door as if to hear if someone was at home or not. Then he knocked softly on the door. Her heart started pounding, then an eerie feeling of fear came over her.

She tried to stay calm for her children. Then wouldn't you know it, they got excited and asked if that was their daddy. June knew then that the guy outside knew someone was home. Her mind raced back and forth. *What would he do now? Will he try to bust through the door? Will he turn and walk away? Will he knock harder until someone opens the door? Will he go around to the back door? Is he alone?*

June slowly opened the door as her mother instincts were on high alert. She placed her right foot behind the door and her right hand was on the door knob while her left hand was on the door frame, just in case he tried to push the door open once she opened it. Her children tried to peep around her to see who was there, so she pushed them back with her left hand.

All of a sudden, June found herself in a very bad situation. She had to place her left leg in a position to block them from trying to look out the door, still keeping her left hand on the door frame and keep her right foot behind the door and her right hand on the door knob. All the while, she kept her eyes on this stranger. But her youngest son was very persistent in trying to see who was at the door which placed her motherly homeland security alert to "critical." Yet June knew she had to stay calm and observant.

At the time she opened the door, she saw a hard-core mischievous look on the stranger's face. Could it be that he didn't hear anything? Then June heard a small voice say, "He's going to try to break in."

Then the man's facial expression changed to shock and panic. His whole posture changed in seconds from attack stance as he looked at June and her children, to that of caution as he held the screen door while facing his car.

June kept her eyes on him as she tried to keep her son from peeping out the door. In seconds, June's mind raced with all types of thoughts: *The construction workers are still at lunch. My neighbors aren't home. If only my husband would pull up right now. I have no idea what this guy's about to do or what he's thinking after seeing me and my children.*

As June looked intently into his beady green eyes, he seemed to melt right before her. She said, "Yes, can I help you?"

He replied hesitantly, "I used to live here. I can't find the home I used to stay in. The number is 346."

She said to herself, *He's lying. We're one of the first families to move into the subdivision and that house number never existed. It surely wasn't here or in front of us.* She looked him dead in the eyes with a stern look and said, "There's no house here with that number."

After that, it seemed as if something went off in his mind and his whole demeanor changed to being hardcore. He quickly turned his body back toward June in an aggressive stance. Suddenly, his attention left June and went straight over her left shoulder. His eyes changed, and they were filled with fear. He quickly turned his body while looking nervously toward his car. He politely said,

"Thank you. I don't know where the house is. I made a mistake." He walked away briskly and quickly drove off.

June quickly closed the door with a sigh of relief and said, "What was that?" She called the front office of the subdivision to alert them of the stranger. She told the office manager what happened, gave a description of the car and the man.

The office manager said, "You are correct, there has never been a house with that number in this subdivision. We will keep an eye out for him. Thank you!"

A flood of emotions hit June, and she called her husband to tell him about her terrifying experience. It was totally out of character for her to open a door up to a stranger. But she felt compel to open the door, she thought the stranger knew they were home. June thanked God for protecting her and her boys from harm. She had no idea what changed the stranger's plans or what he saw over her left shoulder that made him change his mind. But whatever it was, it put fear in his heart and changed his agenda for her and her boys. And hopefully, it put him on the honest track.

Food for thought

What memory or memories came to mind as you read this story? Can you recall at least one time when you were in a situation that could've turned bad because of a choice you made or because of a situation you had no control of? As you look back on it, can you see God's protective hand on your life? Can you remember Him speaking to you or the feeling of Him leading you in a certain direction away from harm's way? Or could you see an individual's whole disposition change for the good right before your eyes?

Scriptures for your soul

> For he will command his angels concerning you to guard you in all your ways. (Ps. 91:11)

See, I am sending an angel ahead of you to guard you along the way and to bring you to the place I have prepared. (Exod. 23:20)

When the donkey saw the angel of the Lord standing in the road with a drawn sword in his hand, it turned off the road into a field. Balaam beat it to get it back on the road. (Num. 22:23)

He will command his angels concerning you to guard you carefully. (Luke 4:10)

But the Lord is faithful, and he will strengthen you and protect you from the evil one. (2 Thess. 3:3)

CHAPTER 5

Patience is a Virtue

Will a couple minutes truly save you or will it be your demise?

It was a beautiful hot summer day in Knoxville. June was working temporarily downtown at city hall. The long day had just ended, and she was about to face the 5:00 p.m. rush hour traffic. All she could think about was getting home to see her sons and her plans for her eldest son's birthday party on Saturday.

June drove a two-door older model car, affectionately named Boomer by her sons.

Boomer had no AC and leather seats. It leaked fluids when it ran hot or if the car stood while on for long periods of time. She always kept a bottle of oil and a jug of water in the trunk. When she got into the car, she manually rolled both windows all the way down and put her purse on the passenger seat.

Today, the traffic was unusually slow, and June became very impatient. She then thought, *I've got a pretty good sense of direction, and I've got to get out of this traffic.*

Her friend Anita lived downtown, and she showed her several different routes to her place. June started remembering a certain part of downtown that could be a shortcut to the interstate, and she would bypass all of this traffic that was going nowhere. Decisions… decisions… What will she do?

The sun was blazing with temperatures in the upper 90s, the sweat was pouring down like a faucet onto her face and back. Then all of a sudden, the thing she dreaded and knew would happen under these conditions happened, the light on the car's console started flashing. Her car was starting to overheat.

June started panicking; she had to do something. Just then, she saw the street that Anita went down or was it the street? There was no more time to lose, so June made a quick decision and made a right turn off the main street that would have eventually taken her straight to the interstate.

She drove down the street feeling relieved that she dodged all that crazy traffic. As she kept driving the surroundings became more and more unfamiliar to her. She was beginning to get a little scared. So June started praying and asked God to show her how to get out of the maze of buildings and apartments. She was going deeper and deeper into unknown, uncharted territory. She kept praying even harder.

People were everywhere! June got nervous because she realized she was now in the projects and nowhere near where her friend lived. June was a young attractive woman, alone in a car with her paycheck in her purse. She became a little paranoid and thought everyone knew she didn't belong. Then she thought, *What would happen to my boys if someone carjacks me and the unthinkable hap-*

53

pens? They'll never find me because no one knows I took this route.

June came to a stop sign; the car on her right side had the right away. The driver hesitated and drove slowly through the intersection as he stared hard at June. This made her really nervous, and she was scared. As this happened, she noticed four extremely loud guys came out of a store.

Then one of the guys started running across the street toward her car, and it looked like he had something white in his hand. She could tell by his behavior and wild eyes as he was quickly approaching the car that he was high on something.

Then her attention went back to the guy in the car in front of her, he slowly made a left turn as he stared her down. June took her eyes off the guy running toward her for a split second to see where the car went. As she turned her head back to the right to see where the guy was, she was startled when she saw that he was standing next to her car. She froze!

He quickly stooped down, looked into the car at her, and then he quickly punched the passenger door really hard and said, "Hey! Stick 'em up!"

She looked straight into those cold dark eyes that looked straight through her. Thoughts zoomed through her mind, going 100 mph. *Did he see my purse and will he grab it and run? Is he gonna jump into my car and my boys would never see me again?*

Then her eyes were drawn to his hand on her window, she saw something white. It was a white handkerchief with the silhouette of a gun underneath. June started praying even harder as her life flashed before her eyes and thought, *Oh my God, what have I done!*

She heard his friends laughing as they were walking across the street toward them, "Man, stop playing." They laughed. "Leave the lady alone!" He looked at them and then looked back at June with his cold dead eyes, and he looked at her purse laying on the seat and then back at her. It was as if a light came on in his mind when his friends called out to him.

June now realized his focus was on her and the car all this time, and he didn't even see her purse. But now, his attention was on the purse that was closer to him than it was to her. Nothing was stopping him from quickly reaching in, grabbing the purse, and running away. Nothing was stopping him from making her get out of the car or jumping into it and telling her to drive off. June felt helpless as she stared into his cold dark eyes. So she did the only thing she could do and that was to pray.

But then the unexpected happened—he looked at his friends again and then back at June. To June surprise, he quickly jumped back away from the car with a terrified expression. She didn't know what he saw at that moment on the passenger seat, but it wasn't the purse anymore. Whatever it was, it terrified him to the point that he was physically shaken! His friends then came over by the car snickering and took the white handkerchief from him, telling him, "Come on and leave the lady alone."

As he was distracted, June sped off! She didn't know if any cars were at the intersection or not. Her heart was racing, and she got out of there! She felt lead to drive straight and then make a right turn. She was finally out!

As she drove out, she remembered something her friend Anita said when they were walking some weeks back, "I might walk all over town, but I know to stay out of that section of town." If only June had remembered that earlier.

June thanked the Lord for once again coming to her rescue. When she got home, she hugged her boys like it was for the very first time or like she hadn't seen them in days!

That Saturday was the best birthday party at Chucky Cheese that she and her son had ever experienced or ever will. One day when he's old enough, June will tell him about the "birthday party that almost never was." But God! And about "a truly merciful and faithful God that protects and watches over us daily, even when we make decisions that place us in bad situations."

Food for thought

What memory or memories came to mind as you read this story? Can you recall at least one time when you were in a situation because of something that you brought upon yourself because you didn't have patience? Can you now see that it wasn't you, and somehow God stepped in, in spite of your impatience, and He rescued you from the unknown? Do you see why having patience is so important?

Scriptures for your soul

> The Lord will fight for you; you need only to be still. (Exod. 14:14)

> Be strong and courageous. Do not be afraid or terrified because of them, for the Lord your God goes with you; he will never leave you nor forsake you. (Deut. 31:6)

> I waited patiently for the Lord; he turned to me and heard my cry. (Ps. 40:1)

God is our refuge and strength, an ever-present help in trouble. (Ps. 46:1)

Whoever dwells in the shelter of the Most High will rest in the shadow of the Almighty. I will say of the Lord, He is my refuge and my fortress, my God, in whom I trust. (Ps. 91:1–2)

The name of the Lord is a fortified tower; the righteous run to it and are safe. (Prov. 18:10)

Be joyful in hope, patient in affliction, and faithful in prayer. (Rom. 12:12)

But the Lord is faithful, and he will strengthen you and protect you from the evil one. (2 Thess. 3:3)

About the Author

Roberta Jackson was born and still resides in Atlanta, Georgia. She has been married to "Maestro" Tyrone Jackson for almost twenty years. A very happy coincidence since she is also a gifted vocalist and song writer.

She has two talented sons, Tommie Grant, III and Isaac Grant, and a wonderful gifted grandson, Jordan Grant.

She is currently employed at one of the oldest African American congregational churches in the United States. Her daily administrative responsibilities mesh well with her desire to work in an environment that seeks to help and serve others.

Roberta was introduced to poetry when she was in the fifth grade and there began her love for writing. As a teenager, she used writing to comfort and encourage others.

Her love for writing never stopped! For over thirty years, Roberta has continued to encourage and minister to herself and to others in both poetry and in song.

When she questions her ability, she remembers her mother speaking life into her just before she passed away from breast cancer. On that night, her mother closed her eyes and let out a joyful laugh, exclaiming, "I can see God is going to use you!"

She has taken up the baton, and she is running the race full speed ahead. Through her faith in God, she believes that He will use her "scenarios" to change lives and bring about deliverance.

Scenario Queen is Roberta's first published work, but as long as she can still hear her mother's joyful words, it will not be her last.

A book of poetry will be coming very soon.